Mud Kitchen in a Day

How to Quickly Get Your Kids Outside, Playing in the Dirt, & Enjoying Creative Play

JASON RUNKEL SPERLING

Copyright © 2015 Jason Runkel Sperling

All rights reserved. No part of this book may be reproduced in any form—except in the case of brief quotations embodied in critical articles or reviews—without permission in writing from Jason Runkel Sperling.

This publication is designed to provide accurate and authoritative information in regard to the subject matter covered. It is sold with the understanding that the author is not engaged in rendering medical or other professional service. If medical or other expert assistance is required, the services of a competent professional person should be sought.

First Print Edition, 2016

www.JasonRunkelSperling.com

ISBN: 978-1534968882

To my wife, Michele. Thanks for coming to the mountains with me to raise our children.

CONTENTS

Introduction 7
   Mud Kitchen Is King of Backyard Toys 11
   Getting Started 13
   Quick Start Guide 21

Grow and Expand Your Mud Kitchen 23
   The Oven 23
   The Dirt 28
   The Spigot 34
   The Sink 39

Going Beyond the Mud Kitchen 44
   Creating Play Spaces 44
   Crafting Rhythm 49
   The Art of the Play-Worker 52
   Using Loose Parts to Extend the Mud Kitchen 55
   Looking Ahead 58
   A Philosophy to Help Make Mud More Child-Centered 59

Resources 61
- Things to Cook With 62
- Ingredients 63
- Loose Parts for the Backyard 66
- Dirt, Play, and Child Development 69
- Giant Mud Kitchen Photo Collection 72
- Examples and Articles of Mud Kitchens 73
- Cheat Sheet 79
- Need Help? 80

About The Author 81

Also by Jason Runkel Sperling 85

INTRODUCTION

I grew up in Boulder, Colorado, where the Rocky Mountains give way to the Great Plains and the sun shines most days. The memories of my childhood are filled with outdoor adventures: rafting, hiking, camping, skiing, surfing, and scuba diving. After spending a couple decades traveling and living around the world, I returned to Boulder with my wife, Michele, to raise our adventurous five-year-old daughter Nyla and our sweet, tentative one-year-old son Silas.

Back on my home turf in Colorado, I was eager to expose my children to the natural wonders that I remembered exploring as a kid. I began taking my children to the woods, lakes, and mountains of the beautiful state. But something wasn't right. I grew increasingly aware that their needs did not align with my adventurous goals. For example, they didn't particularly care if we made it to the summit of a mountain. They preferred to play in the muddy stream banks along the trail. They didn't care if we paddled to a cascading, gurgling tributary. They wanted to make boats from nearby leaves and twigs and sail them off to an imaginary world. They didn't care about mastering the alpine slopes on a pair of skis. They were content to jump off a snow bank in the parking lot.

One early morning, Nyla and I crossed a mountain stream as we hiked up a canyon. When we reached the far side, she stopped and crouched down to pick at the stream bank. I enjoyed watching her pluck at the water's edge, fiddle with sticks, and push pebbles around. Her hands were dirty, and her sneakers gooey with mud and chilly water. After a minute or so, I urged her to get moving. She responded that she didn't want to hike. She wanted to play. With all the work of getting up early, packing backpacks full of supplies, researching and planning, and then driving to the trailhead, it was really disappointing to hear her say she didn't want to hike. She wanted to play. She did not share my dreams. But as I let the waves of dismay pass, I saw how she blossomed with joy and creativity, and remained thoroughly engaged for the next hour.

At that point, I realized I needed to temper my ambitions of introducing my children to goal-oriented and skill-based outdoor adventures. I decided to observe what activities seemed to be the most rewarding for them and then support those activities. Some things are obvious: Sitting in a car seat is no fun for a kid. Mastering an athletic skill or following rules can be rather dull for small children.

It began to dawn on me...why not let the children enjoy unstructured play? Why not just stay home in the backyard?

Today, unstructured play, outdoor experiences, and spaces have been transformed significantly from previous decades. The seemingly unlimited free time children once knew as "childhood" has become dominated by school, extracurricular activities, less spacious lands for wandering freely, and a growing sense of fear in letting children follow their own agenda. Overall, there is simply far less time and freedom for children today to just play. Much free time is oriented to screen-based activities versus free-play outside. Add to this reality the fact that many backyards are manicured and designed for adult enjoyment rather than children's use.

My parents and friends all remember childhoods filled with interactions with the natural world, and that's how I hope my children will remember their early years.

Mud kitchens are not obvious. Until recently, I had never heard of one. They aren't commonly sold in stores or marketed in advertisements. You can make one yourself simply, and for little cost. It doesn't matter the size or condition of a backyard, a mud kitchen can still be made.

A backyard mud kitchen provides a gateway experience that supports children's natural inquisitiveness. It supports their need to develop cognitive, gross, and fine motor skills, and foster their relationship with the outdoors and organic materials—all while giving them a feeling of independence and emotional well-being.

While there is no shortage of information and inspiration about mud kitchens online, I am consistently surprised by how few parents have heard of them. In addition, it is easy to get overwhelmed and reach a state of analysis paralysis, where you make no progress in getting a mud kitchen going for days or months.

My hope with this book is to share my family's mud kitchen creation experience, so that you have the ability to quickly go outside and build your own mud kitchen.

How to Use This Book

This book is organized into three main sections. The first section shares the story of how we created a mud kitchen quickly by adjusting our expectations and design strategy. You will be able to complete this section in the next few minutes and should be equipped at that point to build your mud kitchen. The second and third sections share how you can expand and go beyond your initial mud kitchen creation. Lastly, resources are available for those who want to research more extensively.

Mud Kitchen Is King of Backyard Toys

If you're like I was and have never heard of a mud kitchen, you might be envisioning a sink and a faucet surrounded by mud. And some mud kitchens are composed of just that. Some are more rudimentary, and others are grander. But regardless of how fancy the setup, with just a few simple accoutrements, a mud kitchen for a child presents an elaborate experience, much like an adult's experience creating a feast using an indoor kitchen. Recipes ignite the imagination; spices and ingredients present diverse aromas, textures, and colors; cookware, utensils, and dishes provide the tools and environment in in which to experiment and make mud concoctions. Mud kitchens may occupy a small space in the backyard, but in my experience their boundaries are far-reaching—far more than many toys.

We buy a lot of toys for our children. We have a backyard full of seemingly amazing options: geodesic dome, swing set, teepee, hammock, basket full of balls and lawn games, water table, and full body sand pit. However, the mud kitchen gets more attention than anything else—by a long shot!

My children will play with those other things for a while, but the mud kitchen is king of the backyard toys. My children will play in the mud kitchen for hours and hours. If you are looking for that toy that keeps children entertained in the backyard, a mud kitchen is it!

Beyond getting the highest engagement and making them the happiest of any toy, it is also extremely inexpensive, incredibly valuable for child development, and more fun (in my experience) for the parents.

Getting Started

When we first considered making a mud kitchen, we turned to Google and quickly became overwhelmed by how much effort it would take to set one up. There are some really beautiful mud kitchens out there, the kind built with master carpentry skills and craftsmanship—even artistry.

My Pinterest board has hundreds of examples of mud kitchens, from simple makeshift kitchens to elaborate brilliant works of craftsmanship and imagination. You can find it here:

https://www.pinterest.com/jasonsperling/mud-kitchens/

There are SuperDads—and more likely SuperMoms—out there building mud kitchens that are rustic, iconic, coordinated, and even breathtaking. Their designs are stunning. My favorite ones consist of beautiful wooden counters and shelving, stainless steel fixtures, chalkboards with handwritten menus, baskets of ingredients, farmhouse style buckets, antique cookware, and Hobbit-like furniture featuring aged stumps and twisted tree parts. We wanted that for our children, of course. But there was a hitch: I'm not particularly handy. And, more often that not, I feel pretty crunched for time.

Overwhelmed, my wife and I spent months not starting.

One day, frustrated by how little "digging in the dirt" my children were doing, I rethought my approach. It was a sunny day, and my kids were drifting around the sandbox and lawn. I thought, rather than spending time designing the perfect mud kitchen, what could I get done this morning? How could I involve the kids so they could play right away? Forget SuperDad, I thought. Let's just get something started so they can play now.

I looked around and discovered an old board that we had yet to throw out. It was a bit warped, cracked, and dirty. But it could be sanded. Hmmm...could this be the mud kitchen counter?

Next to the board sat a dilapidated wooden lattice panel. Perhaps it could be the backsplash behind the counter? I walked into the garage. There, I found an old IKEA spice rack with a few hooks for pots and pans, some scrap 2x4s, and a few screws. I called my kids into the garage and we started sanding and assembling rickety, wobbly spare parts to a kid-height counter with a backsplash and hangers to hold buckets. After a few minutes, we were finished.

Both kids helped me carry our creation out to the backyard. We stuck the counter under the deck, a place that would remain cool on hot days, where a patch of dirt had yet to be covered by grass or rock. The counter was pretty unstable, so we piled some rocks and dirt by the legs to help it stand on its own. It still wasn't very stable, so we tied it to one of the deck legs. Then we went to the sandbox and gathered a few buckets that we filled with water from a nearby garden spigot.

This was where things really took off. Returning to the counter, I sat down and nonchalantly showed my kids how to make a mud pie. It had been less than an hour, and we had a fully functioning mud kitchen! I felt like I had cracked open the secret to the universe...or at least the secret to keeping my kids entertained outside. The kids played for hours that day, and we all left feeling proud and excited about our new creation.

Nyla and Silas playing on the counter in the mud kitchen, constructed from spare 2x4s, unused board, lattice, and IKEA kitchen hanger.

If you don't have spare parts hanging around your house, you can still get started right away. Children's imaginations are vast. The ingredients for a mud kitchen are really minimal:

1. Dirt

2. Water

3. Something to "cook" in

If you have a very manicured lawn, dig a hole in the corner of the yard, removing a patch of grass to access the dirt beneath. You can mix sand with potting soil. You can pick up buckets of fill dirt, potting soil, and sand from local landscaping companies or hardware shops like Home Depot. If you don't have outdoor spigots, you can supply water from your house. You also might not have play buckets handy, in which case you can use Tupperware or any pots and pans from your indoor kitchen. Mud isn't going to ruin them.

With those three ingredients you can build a mud kitchen and provide endless hours of entertainment. Tell the children what you're building so they can start to create their own mental model. They'll quickly begin to add things to the mud kitchen using their imagination, and gathering things from the yard. If they don't immediately begin this process, your job as a play-worker (more on that later) is to model for them.

Here are some easy ways to get the children playing:

Unpack the Kitchen

A kitchen needs all sorts of utensils and bake ware. Help your child think about what he or she will need in the kitchen. For example, you may say, "Hmmm...I need a spoon" as you walk around the yard searching for a stick. Find a forked stick? A perfect blender! Create a stove by gathering a few stones or bricks and arranging them in such a way that you can set your pot upon them. Want a four-burner top? Get more rocks. Big leaves are great for napkins or pot holders. Just think through what is in your real kitchen, and go hunting for it in the yard. Get creative! If you can't find it, don't worry—just move on. Soon the children will be following your lead, and you can go back to the cooking.

Make Different Foods

Every dish has a unique recipe that requires all sorts of food, but also spices. Yards make great places for gathering spices in the form of flower petals, grass clippings, weeds, seedpods, bark, and sand and soil of different colors and textures. My children had a blast gathering these items and creating a collection in different containers. If your yard doesn't have a wealth of organic materials, you can make a special trip to a nearby park, open space, or friend's yard to collect a few handfuls.

Decorate the Dining Room

After the kitchen is done, the dining room needs work. Think about how you might set the table for a grand dinner party. Things like candles, flowers, place settings, centerpieces, coasters, cups, and bowls are all exciting to search for in the yard. Some items from inside the house can also be dedicated to the mud kitchen. Keep it simple but fun.

Measuring the Ingredients

Pouring sand and water (or anything, really) is a surprisingly engaging task for young children. With just a few different sized containers, kids can start measuring and counting. No one is watching to see if they follow the recipe, so encourage them to vary their quantities and use measuring cups or spoons frequently. If you happen to lose count, start all over. Keep in mind that repetitive play is how children build and master skills.

Get Muddy!

With how safe and sterile play has become in the recent decades, it may be that your child hasn't experienced the joy of getting muddy. If they don't spontaneously start getting all muddy—and I mean from head to toe—then you can encourage this behavior by painting mud on your arm or your face, saying, "Cooking sure is messy!" My wife wasn't so sure she wanted Mud Monsters for children, but the fastest way to ruin the fun would be requiring children to keep clean in the mud kitchen. I quickly hose them down when they are done and strip them out of their muddy clothes or swimsuits, and my wife is a happy camper. Happy kids. Happy wife.

I have heard of some folks who have children wear aprons.

If you'd like to do that, you can find some pleasant ones at CommunityPlaythings.com.

What Age Is Right?

Now you might be wondering what age is appropriate for mud kitchen play. As with so many things, it depends. By the time we started the mud kitchen, our children were no longer putting everything in their mouths, so eating the mud wasn't an issue. Besides eating mud, if children throw or wipe mud on themselves, it can get into their eyes, ears, nose, etc. I kept close tabs on my children in the beginning to make sure the mud kitchen did not present any risk. Silas began playing in the mud kitchen when he was around 20 months and we never experienced any issues.

Quick Start Guide

Here are some things to think about when crafting your mud kitchen:

- Construct furniture, fixtures, and the space at child height.

- Incorporate multiple levels or work surfaces, doors, and things for hanging.

- Set it directly in or next to the supply of dirt and other organic materials.

- Locate it in shade or partial shade if hot summer days discourage play.

- Provide self-serve water nearby for play.

- Establish other areas within the yard as part of the mud kitchen experience.

- Use real kitchen tools and model real cooking behavior.

- Include tools across a spectrum of function: stirring, scooping, pouring, mixing, baking, washing, etc.

- Forage in advance if ingredients are not easily accessible.

- Avoid elaborate designs or using new materials to remove barriers to starting.

- Design the kitchen for multiple children so friends can easily participate.

- Avoid soil or areas with chemicals or dangerous construction debris.

- Ensure an outside water source for easy cleanup.

GROW AND EXPAND YOUR MUD KITCHEN

The following section dives into different ways that we expanded the mud kitchen. These are not necessary, but we found they enhanced the overall experience. As you'll discover, these were all added over time in a very iterative fashion. To this day we are still observing, experimenting, and evolving the mud kitchen.

The Oven

One day, Nyla and I were walking to our local grocery store and saw a worn-down wooden coffee table on the sidewalk. Taped on the front was a handwritten sign that read "Antique $40." We stopped and looked at it. It was unusual with a large enclosed shelf under the tabletop and a door that ran the length of the shelf and opened downward. It seemed too big to go anywhere inside our house, but the door opened the same as an oven. I suggested it could be a good oven for the mud kitchen, but $40 seemed too much money to spend on our experimental mud kitchen that we had made from scrap materials in our yard and garage. So we walked on to the store. On our way home, the sign was now flipped over and had the word "FREE!" written on it. Nyla and I were both really excited. I told her that, if she wanted it, we would have to carry it back home together.

Nyla examining an antique desk offered for free on the curb as a candidate for the mud kitchen.

She excitedly grabbed one edge, and we began to walk it back a couple of blocks. It was slow going with many stops, but we finally arrived at our backyard and proudly put the oven into the mud kitchen.

Nyla promptly began cooking. She cooked mud pancakes on the surface of the table and then put mud pies and cakes (buckets of mud) into the oven. Periodically, she checked on the food in the oven to see if it was cooked.

Gathering Fixtures and Equipment

Over the summer, I found that one of the enjoyable aspects of the mud kitchen was sourcing fixtures like the oven. While you may want to purchase some new and used furniture for the mud kitchen, there is a romantic and charming quality in building it over time and through serendipity.

You can get fixtures and equipment from:

- Garage sales
- Free stuff on sidewalks or websites
- Stores or marketplaces

Garage Sales

Garage sales are one of my favorite ways to find things for the mud kitchen. I started visiting garage sales with Nyla early in the summer. We would not make a special trip or go garage sale hunting. Rather, if we were out on the town and happened to see a sign for a garage sale, we would drop by. Sometimes we would go to a few in one day. We moved very fast, looking for specific things like a new table, chair, or bucket. It was really fun for Nyla because I would prompt and support her doing the talking and negotiating. After a few weeks of that, and ever since, Nyla gets very excited whenever she sees a sign for a garage sale. Like shrieking excited! I'll ask her what she needs, and it is usually something for the mud kitchen. This makes for a pretty fun way to experience the city and interact with the community. It also allows Nyla to be the architect of the mud kitchen, which is something she doesn't usually get to do around our home. And, of course, the cost of getting fixtures this way is very low, especially because you don't need something of high quality. For example, one of the items we purchased at a garage sale was a narrow coffee table that we turned into a sink, and it cost only $5.

Free Stuff on Sidewalks

We keep our eyes out for whenever there is free stuff sitting on the side of the road, as we did with the oven. Like garage sales, this is a pretty fun diversion in the middle of our day. We'll stop to check something out, and Nyla can be the judge of whether or not it is a good fit. You can also tell friends and family about your mud kitchen and what types of things you're on the lookout for. They may have something they are no longer using that they'd be happy to donate to your mud kitchen. There is a plethora of websites these days that list free things (e.g., Craigslist.com or NextDoor.com). And never underestimate the value of organic material; sticks and branches make for great cookware, and stones and boulders can make for good pans or benches. These can be collected from your yard or forest service areas.

Both garage sales and free stuff add a rich tone to the mud kitchen experience because the creation of the mud kitchen happens in part by chance and good fortune. It adds a certain feeling of luck and magic to the creation, not to mention a bit of randomness to the space.

Stores or Marketplaces

Hardware stores, toy shops, kitchen supply stores, and secondhand stores are important places to source inexpensive equipment like buckets, shovels, spoons, various fixtures, etc. if you don't have them already. I bought a couple of large, galvanized steel buckets to add to our collection of sand toy buckets, and these have been great for hauling dirt and water. I suggest you get buckets big enough for children to step into!

It's fun to visit these kinds of stores with your child, but if you are pressed for time or trying to source something that your local stores don't carry, you can purchase products online from Internet marketplaces. There are a vast number of stores that have online platforms. Places like eBay.com and Etsy.com are great to find vintage, handmade, and used products. On these sites, I've seen beautiful, custom-designed mud kitchens using wood pallets and reclaimed sinks outfitted with hose attachments. They are pricey (as is any custom-built furniture), but would make for a wonderful play space.

The Dirt

We first built the mud kitchen in early April. It was during a typical warm spell that we see here in Boulder, and so when it snowed later in the month, it presented a rather amusing few days for the mud kitchen. The conditions were perfect for making snowballs, and Nyla and I ended up making dozens of them. Then she proceeded to put them into the mud kitchen's oven. Later in the day, Silas came out and both children continued to fill the oven up.

Nyla and Silas placing "snow" balls in the newly acquired oven during a spring snow day.

When the warm temperatures returned, I noticed that she wasn't doing the same with mud. Initially I couldn't figure out why, and then I tried myself. The dirt she was using was from the ground, but it was mixed with small quantities of gravel and sand, grasses, weeds, and other organic bits and pieces. It was ideal for making soups and even pancakes, but mud balls? Nope. The mud just kind of fell apart.

Just east of town there is a sand and gravel company named *Pioneer*. It's a fun place to visit with the kids because there are giant two-story mounds of all sorts of sand, gravel, dirt, mulch, and rocks. We visited and explained our challenge to the folks in the office. Not surprisingly, they didn't know exactly what would work, but recommended we check out some fill dirt that had a bit of a clay-like consistency to it. We drove over to the mound and tested it. The dirt was dry, but we were able to pack balls of it that stayed together slightly. We gathered a couple buckets worth and brought it home. Back at the mud kitchen, Nyla proceeded to combine small amounts of the new dirt with water. And presto! We were able to make smooth, beautiful mud. When thick enough, we could easily pack the mud into balls. In the next hour, we filled the oven full of mud balls to let them cook. The next day, the mud balls were dry, almost as hard as rocks.

While the folks over at Happy Hooligans have experimented with using potting soil and sand at a ratio or 2:1 to achieve a usable "mud," I've experimented with a number of different dirt types and found that getting good mud is important.

For those who want to pick up the dirt yourself, you may be able to get it for free from construction or excavation companies or from homeowners or other businesses posting online (on Craigslist, for example). If you purchase from landscaping or sand and gravel companies, the cost of dirt varies greatly by location. These companies will load your truck, trailer, or their own dump truck, and they sell by cubic yard or ton. So, when we fill up a five-gallon bucket of dirt, we get some pretty funny looks and the bill usually comes to around $10 or less. Once they even told us to take the dirt for free! If you buy in bags from home improvement stores (like HomeDepot), the cost will sometimes be higher, but not always.

How to Find the Good Mud

- It should be fine grained (without much debris in it) and feel good in your hands when dry, with a clay-like texture to it.

- When combined with water, it makes a smooth blend like what you might find at a mud spa.

- As it thickens, you should be able to press it together to make balls that can be set out to dry.

Higher quality mud leads to an expanded set of play opportunities.

Mix

Having completely dry dirt offers children the chance to experiment with mixing dirt and water to make mud at a varying degree of thicknesses. If you've ever allowed your children to help "cook" in the home kitchen, it is amazing how engaged they can be creating a soup or potion from scratch. With dry dirt, a water source, and a yard to pick things from, the mud kitchen can be an experimental lab that vigorously captures their attention. It's useful to have a variety of pots, pans, pitchers, ladles, and other scooping, pouring, and mixing devices to help aid in this process. When the dry dirt source runs out, I've noticed the play changes quite a bit, so having an ongoing supply of dry dirt can be helpful.

Reconstitute

After a mud ball, soup, or pancake dries, it starts to lose its utility. They really can dry as hard as a rock and then can't be played with in quite the same way. However, you can put these dried out pieces of mud into a bucket with other mud or water and start the process over again. As a play-worker, you can assist in this process if you notice pieces of mud or surfaces covered in thick mud that are not being used. Just scrape or pick the mud up and put it into liquid, giving the children the source material again.

Make Dirt

Another option for dried-up mud is to crush it back into fine dirt. Almost any surface and set of tools can work. This is another activity that can be expanded on in so many ways. For example, you can find a variety of stones and sticks and hammer-like rods and other tools to assist in the process. Strainers and sifting cookware can help the children focus on producing the finest of dirt grains. This is hard, important work, and the newly created dirt can be collected in special containers and reserved for toppings of mud pies or as the special ingredient for a soup being made for a yard festival.

Even Simpler

Make a mobile mud kitchen! Use a wheelbarrow or other garden cart and have a mud kitchen that can be moved about versus being installed permanently.

Visit this blog post for some sweet inspiration: http://happyhooligans.wordpress.com/2011/08/28/mud-glorious-mud/.

Silas removing handfuls of mud, which has returned to dry fill dirt.

The Spigot

One of our garden spigots is located on the edge of a raised area where an apple tree and maple tree grow. Four stacked railroad ties make up the edges, creating a wall that is three or four feet in height. While there's another spigot closer to the house, Nyla and Silas gravitated to this spigot to fill their buckets. The spigot is not easy to turn, and every time they go about trying to turn it on, I get a little nervous. If they lose their balance, they could topple right over the edge of the wall. Falling from that height is one of the most dangerous risks in the backyard. The spigot isn't easy to turn on, and turning off is just as challenging. Most times, Nyla and Silas would end up leaving the spigot on—if not full blast, then still a good trickle.

To avoid the risk and keep the water from running all day, I found myself constantly running over to help them or urging them (through much protest) to use the spigot closer to the house that was easy to access without any risk of falling over a wall. One day I decided to visit the local hardware shop, to see if I could find a better solution. I found an attachment to the spigot that allowed the children to squeeze a lever to turn on the water; when released, the water turned off automatically. Perfect! I installed the attachment on the spigot closest to the house. Now, Nyla and Silas can carry buckets or pitchers over to this spigot, turn the water on themselves, and simply walk away. The water turns itself off. This immediately made their experience much more independent and self-reliant. They were able to play without needing my help and could self-direct how the day went without adult intervention. It also made our yard safer and more relaxing for me.

36   Mud Kitchen in a Day

Nyla fills a bucket with the newly added self-closing spigot attachment.

Creating a Self-Serving Water Source

- Find an attachment to an existing spigot that can be turned on with a lever, and that, when released, automatically turns off.

- Get a sprayer hose attachment that can be left on that works in a similar way and is easy to operate.

- Fill a large holding tank full of water that the children can dip their buckets into.

- Get a five-gallon or seven-gallon blue water container with a spigot and put that in back.

While this equipment will likely need to be purchased from a hardware or garden supply store, it enhances the play experience in several ways.

Independent Play

It's worth mentioning again that child-led play is fundamental to children's growth. It gives them the freedom to control their experience by eliminating many of the adult-led rules and guidelines. They direct their minute-by-minute interactions, from playing with dirt and mud to retrieving the water necessary for their experiments.

Motor Skills

Without adult intervention, the children will natural tend toward trying different methods for retrieving water. If you maintain a collection of buckets and pitchers in different sizes, the children will naturally fill the containers up too full and discover the challenges in keeping the water they've collected instead of spilling it. With very large buckets, they'll end up filling them with too much water, making for a good physical challenge that will engage them over and over as they fill the bucket with too much water, spill, and refill, until they learn their own strength.

Discovering Unintended Uses

While the water is needed for making mud, it has all sorts of other fun uses that as a parent you might not immediately present. Children will explore how water travels across the mud kitchen, nearby landscape, and themselves. They'll use large buckets as small versions of swimming pools perfect for getting their feet into. Allowing water to be plentiful, the children will concoct mixtures of varying degrees of muddiness. One of my favorite moments in the mud kitchen was watching my children fill a bucket far too full with water. They ended up with very diluted muddy water, so Silas proceeded to get into the bucket, sit down on the rim, and start "washing" his hands over and over. Nyla quickly joined him in a second bucket, and both children laughed and giggled and had a quintessential childhood moment. Had I simply carried the heavy bucket over to be a supply source for their mud mixing, this would not have transpired.

Silas washing his hands while sitting on the lip of a galvanized bucket. Nyla joining in the fun and dancing in the bucket of mud.

The Sink

One soggy evening, after finishing the dishes after dinner, we went outside to see how the rainy day had transformed our backyard. After checking on flower pots, the bird pond, and the damp sandbox, the children gravitated over to the mud kitchen. Water pooled in a sink we had made months ago. Nyla made the discovery first, shrieked, and quickly grabbed a nearby broom and proceeded to stir up the contents in the basin: water and sediment. The sediment quickly clouded the water, making for a muddy concoction. The lattice above the nearby counter caught her attention, and she dipped the broom deep into the sink and then pranced over to the lattice and began to paint it.

Galloping—literally galloping—from across the yard in bright green rain boots, Silas charged to the sink. He swirled his hands in it for a moment, then he looked across the mud kitchen searching for something. Nothing seemed to register, and so he bent over and tried to pry open the oven. Nyla helped him dislodge the door, and inside he found what he was looking for: a stainless steel toy pot. Silas dipped the pot into the muddy sink water. Lifted it. Poured it back. And then he did that another couple dozen times, with Nyla weaving between pours to refill the paint on her brush to complete her refurbishing of the lattice.

After a counter, a sink in the mud kitchen is probably the next best piece of furniture that we've added.

Silas doing dishes in the homemade sink.

Benefits of a Sink

- Provides a safe place for water to reside (that younger ones can't accidentally trip and fall into).

- Builds on the mental model of the mud kitchen being an actual kitchen, as a sink is one of the defining features of kitchens.

- Introduces several new behaviors for children to model, including washing dishes, washing hands, drying dishes, and pouring and filling containers.

There are a variety of ways to make a sink.

Low-Fidelity

If you aren't handy or want to get started right away, the easiest way to make a sink is just to find any flat container, fill it with water, and put it on the ground or on some raised stand and pronounce that it is a sink. The children will respond well to this, and the only real challenge will be keeping it steady, which may or may not be too severe of a problem depending on the size/stability of the container, location, and how vigorously your children play with it. Of course, you can experiment with using five-gallon buckets and other deeper types of containers, but those are more difficult for small hands and arms to reach compared to shallow dishes.

Modifying Found Materials

The first sink that we created was inspired after we had already obtained the materials. Nyla had searched garage sales for months to find a table and chairs to add as the dining room for the mud kitchen. She found a rickety coffee table and bought it for $5. Michele had purchased some antique ceramic refrigerator drawers (about 9" x 13" x 4" pans) that we used for doing dishes when camping and around the house at times for various things. One day, the children were using the drawer as a sink sitting on top of the coffee table, and we saw how unstable it was. Since the drawer had a lip on it, I cut a hole in the surface of the coffee table on one side, making for an awesome sink and counter for a drying rack.

There are a lot of ways to do this—just find furniture that can support things, and containers that hold water, and figure out how to combine the two.

Professional Sink

The other option is to either purchase a pre-made sink or design one to build from scratch. These may turn out to be more aesthetically pleasing than the low-fidelity or modifying found materials option.

Places like CommunityPlaythings.com have a wide selection of wooden furniture for play kitchens that are modular and can be used in an outdoor kitchen. I saw a sink there for a couple hundred dollars.

For an inspiring example of someone who built a sink with running water, visit Teacher Tom's blog (http://teachertomsblog.blogspot.com/2010/08/our-mud-pie-kitchen.html).

GOING BEYOND THE MUD KITCHEN

Creating Play Spaces

With the self-serve water in place, the rhythm of the mud kitchen expanded as the children moved between the counter, oven, dirt sources, and spigot. Buckets of water were filled, retrieved, and carried over to the workstations. On one particular sunny day, Nyla ventured far across the lawn, past the orchard to an untended area of the yard with long growing grasses, weeds, and tree offshoots. She found a rock exposed above the grasses and piled some mud balls on it. Silas naturally followed, but the ground was irregular and difficult for him to move through. I searched the yard and found some flagstone to make a temporary path into the grasses for an easier entrance. As the mud balls piled up, I decided to stack a few flagstones on top of each other in a half circle, making another surface for the children to place mud upon.

As the mud dried and more mud came, this new area became part of the regular rhythm. The children were using the surface as a drying rack and for processing the dried mud balls back into fine dirt. When they needed more dirt supplies for the mud kitchen, they would journey across the lawn and past the orchard to the drying rack, then return to the mud kitchen and head to the spigot to fill their buckets with water. While we still had to replenish our dirt supplies every now and then, this made for a sort of sustainable ecosystem where the children could facilitate and experience the different states and activities of the mud and yard. Near the drying rack they would also collect dried grasses, weeds, and leaves. Where before they might spend the bulk of a playtime in one area of the yard, now more and more of the yard earned their attention.

Temporary path to the drying rack.

Top view of the drying rack—several pieces of flagstone stacked and placed in a sunny spot in the yard.

Creating different play spaces is valuable. Here's what to consider:

- Having the mud kitchen in an area with partial cover helps encourage long play times without being exposed to direct sun for too long.

- Locating the water source some distance away encourages physical challenges and the experience of transporting heavy materials.

- Finding other areas in the yard that can provide drying areas and other sources of organic material increases the range of physical movement and interest in the yard.

Once you have different areas established, you can help children by modeling different behaviors.

Assigning Importance

The care you take in creating play spaces will help signal to children the importance of a play space. While establishing self-serve water, drying racks, or an organic sourcing area, you can take a little extra time to build the space. You can cut away bushes, vines, grasses, etc. to make a clear path and area for the space. Adding some rocks (such as a pile of flagstone or river rock) to outline and accentuate the space creates a visual queue that this is a designated play space. Encouraging the children to create makeshift signage is fun, imbues children with a sense of ownership, and designates the space as part of the home that is valued by the whole family. Nyla helped "paint" and decide on the location for the mud kitchen sign. While it is barely legible to adults, her mental model of the space is greatly increased.

Modeling Play Behavior

Once the play spaces are created, you can demonstrate examples of how to interact in the new space. You can take a break from the mud kitchen, exclaim to the children that "you need more water" or "need to put this mud pie into the drying rack," and then proceed to do so. They may not follow instantly, but with a few examples they'll begin to copy your behavior and soon discover their own approaches.

Introduction Reminders

It is helpful to remind the children of their available play spaces and options at various points throughout the summer. You can prompt them with questions like, "Do you need to dry that now?" or "It looks like you might need more fresh dirt," and remind them where to go to get that. Simple cues like this can help them build their courage or just simply remind them of what they've done in the past. Early in the mornings after breakfast, if I am looking for a way to get them excited to go outside, I'll say something like, "I need to go check on my mud to see if it is dry," or "I think I better get some more water ready for the mud kitchen." Sharing your intentions this way will remind them of how much fun they've had previously, and get them out there.

Crafting Rhythm

One sunny day, the children took to painting themselves with mud from head to toe, and I began to wonder how I would clean them. Their clothes were soaked and brown; they had stepped in buckets of mud, making their shoes filthy dirty; and even their hair had become objects of their mud affection. Years ago, we had bought a small baby pool made up of two halves and an umbrella. The umbrella was long gone, but the plastic shells were still sitting in our storage area. I pulled them out and set them on the lawn. I began to fill them up, yet the water was still chilly. I decided to fill a few bucket loads of water from the hot tub to warm up the water in the pools.

After a bit more playing in the mud kitchen, the children turned to the pools. They barely fit into the baby pools at this point, but they sat down in them and began splashing. Soon they had taken off their clothes, and we used the pools to wash their pants and shirts and shoes, placing them each to dry on the lawn. We had a slip-and-slide that was rarely used, but I set that up. Friends came over and joined in the fun. The children oscillated between the mud kitchen, the pools, and the slip-and-slide. The sun shone warmer and warmer, and we broke out the hose with a crummy but exciting fountain attachment. Usually we'd keep the water on with medium pressure, making the fountain spray up a few feet. But that day we opened the pressure up full blast, spraying the water up high. Eventually, the wind kicked up, chilling the children, and they made their way to the hot tub.

Over the remainder of the summer, we kept the pools available, and a sort of rhythm emerged, as the children would spend hours in the mud kitchen. As the day warmed, they made their way to the pools. The rhythm made for a predictable play pattern, and the children were free to get as muddy as they wanted.

There are a variety of options for introducing deeper waters into the mud-kitchen experience:

- Find or buy inexpensive inflatable or hard plastic pools.
- Create backyard ponds or streams.
- Buy backyard fountains or hose attachments that can create wide and high sprays of water.

Introducing water features allows the children a new sense of freedom.

Bring on the Mud

They can get as muddy as they want, knowing that they'll have plenty of opportunity for cleaning up.

Washing

Washing muddy clothes outside is surprisingly fun. The children love it.

Managing Water

Having durable water features give children a sense of independence and allows them to interact in new ways.

Nyla spraying mud off her feet using a hose attachment.

The Art of the Play-Worker

"Decades of research have shown that play is crucial to physical, intellectual and social-emotional development at all ages. This is especially true of the purest form of play: the unstructured, self-motivated, imaginative, independent kind, where children initiate their own games and even invent their own rules."

– Dr. David Elkind, *The Power of Play.*

Try to craft the conditions for child-led play, where the child sets the agenda and you, the adult, take a more supportive and distanced role. This is different than adult-led play, where the adult sets rules the child is to follow or where the adult follows the child and interacts directly with the play. In order for children to use play for development, they must be the ones experiencing the various types of play. Thus, in child-led play, the play-worker does not interrupt the child, but does still have some responsibilities.

This has informed my approach with the mud kitchen in a large way.

Play-worker job duties:

- Create and maintain a safe play environment.

- Develop a space filled with prompts for exploratory, imaginative, and creative play.

- Allow children to follow their own agenda rather than adult urges.

- Observe from a distance, letting them move about physically on their own.

- Act (upon request) as a character in their role-playing.
- Introduce new ideas through questions or briefly modeling play behavior.

Put simply, don't "play with" your child. Instead, think of yourself as an architect working to create a space that will help those within it discover their greatest potential. The design (of which you are a part) is most successful if it is not noticed and fades into the tapestry of the walls and corridors. I've found the greatest strides come when there are failures. Being quiet and removed allows me to observe when the children are hitting walls where their play is stinted. When their water sources run dry or when their dirt is all gone, the nature of the play changes, and it's evident what's needed. When the space is too small for multiple children, you can see what's needed. The job of the play-worker is almost counter-intuitive. When I have a weekend to spend with my children, my instinct is to play with them, but their experience is enriched when my job is focused on enabling their play, independently.

Using Loose Parts to Extend the Mud Kitchen

Child-play experts and the people who design play spaces for children have been influenced greatly by the theory of "loose parts," first proposed by architect Simon Nicholson in 1972. Nicholson believed that it is the loose parts in our environment that empower creativity and enrich play. The theory of loose parts says, "In any environment, both the degree of inventiveness and creativity, and the possibility of discovery, are directly proportional to the number and kind of variables in it."

You can read Nicholson's paper here:

http://ojs.lboro.ac.uk/ojs/index.php/SDEC/article/view/1204/1171.

Loose parts have, by definition, no fixed use; these items tend to really work in a modular sense with other loose parts. They may or may not be used in the way you would expect, but are great for stimulating creative, imaginative play scenarios. The following are some examples of loose parts that can augment your play space. You may find the children naturally gravitate toward using them in conjunction with the mud kitchen. Unlike many closed-loop toys (for example, a Brio train set), these have great interoperability. We've introduced many of these into our backyard with great success.

The children posing for a picture while playing with tree slices, tree stumps, and apple tree branches in the background. These loose parts are moveable by the children, and often become the chairs, tables, and walls for fine dining served up from the mud kitchen.

Thinking about and starting to add loose parts to your backyard or play space can quickly transform the space to look a bit junky. When I first started researching loose parts, the rabbit hole seemed to lead to adventure playgrounds. These are numerous in Europe and in the United States. The defining characteristic uniting them is that they do embody a bit of an unappealing aesthetic, especially for adults. I found that my wife quickly became disenchanted with how our backyard began to look as more loose parts appeared.

Fortunately, one of the key principles of loose parts is that the items are transient. You can introduce them and, after a few weeks, clean them up and then later replace them with additional ones. This aligns well with how we've been creating the mud kitchen. The things we've added over periods of time, such as stumps, tree branches, straw bales, tires, etc., get quickly incorporated into the play. Once removed or replaced by other loose parts, they are not missed or detrimental to the child's perception of the space.

In the Resources section you can find my current list of loose parts that I'm experimenting with in our backyard.

Looking Ahead

We're having a lot of fun in our mud kitchen, alone and with friends. We've added a cupboard and a few pots, pans, and other cookware. We've also run into new problems that we're trying to solve.

The children seem to want to play in the mud kitchen daily, which means muddy, muddy children. We're on the lookout for a more permanent hose setup that will allow the children to shower themselves off before coming back into the house. Maybe this will take the shape of a foot shower or similar fixed-water source.

Friends are coming over more frequently and wanting to play in the mud kitchen. We need to add space and things to cook with. We have only a fraction of what you might find in a real kitchen, so there is a lot of opportunity to add new elements.

The children's cooking is becoming more elaborate, and a wider range of ingredients could expand their experience. Our yard and nearby open spaces present a lot of opportunities for foraging, but we'll need containers to hold different ingredients.

And this is just the tip of the iceberg for what's possible....

While I continue to take my children hiking, mountain biking, camping, boating, and exploring open spaces for regular, unstructured nature outings, I consistently find that the backyard mud kitchen experience and play is well suited for them now.

A Philosophy to Help Make Mud More Child-Centered

For those who appreciate philosophical approaches to life and parenting, a helpful concept to keep in mind is one from Taoism—wu wei, or non-action. Wu wei refers to cultivating a way of being in which our actions are aligned with the natural ebb and flow of cycles in the natural world. Think of it like "going with the flow," where your efforts are approached with effortlessness. By surrendering control of how you want the mud kitchen to be and instead focusing on how to react to the present moment, you can enjoy a very pleasant and rewarding interaction with your community, as well as a transition of materials between neighbors and your own home. You will find, in my experience, a real joy in building something without strict guidelines, judgment, or the common framework of our consumer-oriented culture. But most importantly, being open to creating a mud kitchen based on how everyday experiences can shape it provides an unexpected, inspirational, and engaging play space for your child.

One of the biggest challenges in creating a mud kitchen is the process of keeping an ego-less approach at your center. If you can start with nothing more than a hole in the ground, a pot, and a concept, you will be doing well for yourself and your child. Add a board or two and a few other ingredients and accouterments, and you'll be off to a great start.

Fail fast may be a motto typically reserved for software developers and entrepreneurs, but it is relevant in these efforts as well. I have found that worrying less about the presentation and more about the outcome has provided years of fertile learning and development opportunities for my children.

So go ahead and get dirty!

RESOURCES

The print version of *Mud Kitchen in a Day* does not include links to research and resources cited in the following sections that appear as hyperlinks in the digital version.

For these links, please visit:

http://www.MudKitcheninaDay.com.

Silas scoops "hot cereal" carefully from the blue bucket to the terracotta bucket.

Things to Cook With

As we've been thinking about this summer, I've started keeping lists of inspiration from others. Here is a collection of some of the best ideas that might inspire you.

Kitchenware, Utensils, and Tools

- Pots, pans, cooking tins
- Large metal or plastic bowls
- Cooking utensils (the sturdier the better!)
- Recycled containers
- Recipe cards, pencils, recipe box
- Cookbooks
- Canisters to hold different kinds of dirt
- Drainer for dishes
- Sifter, colander
- Towels, dishrags, pot holders
- Spice shakers
- Condiment containers

Fixtures and Accessories

- Crates
- Old tables
- End tables (they can act as stoves and fridges)
- Wooden spoons
- Small pots and pans
- Shiny dishes
- Jell-O molds
- Measuring spoons and cups
- Buckets
- Large tub (to act as a sink)
- Nearby hose
- Tree slices

Ingredients

Besides high-quality dirt that can be turned into mud, you can collect a variety of other landscaping, natural, household, and food items. Taking time to place these in containers, buckets, emptied spice shakers, and jars makes them easy to access for children. You can go on both indoor and outdoor foraging trips with your children to collect these ingredients. Foraging, organizing, and ultimately cooking with a wide range of ingredients provides a rich sensory experience for children.

Food

- Coffee grounds (preferably unused or dried)
- Eggshells (crushed and tinted in different colors)
- Herbs (fresh, dried)
- Orange peel
- Water that is tinted in different colors (using natural food dyes like turmeric, beets, etc.)

Landscaping and Household

- Glass pebbles
- Mulch (different textures and colors)
- Sand (colored and plain)
- Sawdust

- Stones (different sizes and colors)

Natural

- Bark
- Grass
- Leaves (dried and crushed into bits)
- Pebbles
- Pine cones
- Reeds
- Seeds
- Shells
- Stones
- Twigs
- Woodchips

When I started our mud kitchen, we just included dirt, sand, and whatever natural ingredients the children were able to collect from the yard.

If you're not sure how these other ingredients might contribute to a mud kitchen, check out the board I created on Pinterest:

(https://www.pinterest.com/jasonsperling/mud-kitchens/) for some inspiration.

Loose Parts for the Backyard

Tree Parts

- Stumps
- Slices
- Logs
- Poles
- Rough-cut boards
- Smaller sticks
- Leaves
- Mulch

Rocks, Sand, Dirt

- River stones (fairly smooth "pebbles" about four to six inches)
- Flagstone of various dimensions and weights
- Pea gravel
- Boulders

- Pavers
- Bricks
- Dirt
- Sand

Joiners

- Rope
- Cable ties
- Inner tubes of bicycles (cut into lengths with the valve cut out)
- Pulleys
- String
- Cord

Household

- Bandages
- Pots and pans
- Muffin tins
- Plastic containers
- Wooden spoons

- Lattice
- Wood home renovation materials (4x4s, 2x4s, plywood, siding, etc.)

Textile-type materials

- Cushions
- Sheets
- Drop cloths
- Towels
- Blankets

Transportation

- Child-size wheelbarrow
- Buckets
- Wagons
- Car tires
- Rope and pulley

Dirt, Play, and Child Development

Silas enjoying a mud footbath at the children's pop-up spa behind the mud kitchen.

There's a plethora of research and information about the benefits of play, play in nature, and how playing in the mud enhances child development. Here are some of my favorite resources:

Depressed? Go Play in the Dirt, Livescience

This is a study that discusses bacteria called Mycobacterium vaccae, which is good for your brain. The bacteria naturally found in soil increases levels of serotonin, helping to relax, soothe, calm, and help make you feel happy.

Einstein Never Used Flashcards: How Our Children Really Learn—and Why They Need to Play More and Memorize Less, Kathy Hirsh-Pasek, Ph.D. and Roberta Michnick Golinkoff, Ph.D., with Diane Eyer, Ph.D.

A book that explains the process of learning from a child's point of view, including the five elements of play:

Play must be pleasurable and enjoyable.

Play must have no extrinsic goals; there is no prescribed learning that must occur.

Play is spontaneous and voluntary.

Play involves active engagement on the part of the player.

Play involves an element of make-believe.

The Adult Role in Child-led Play – How to Become a Learning Ally, NaturePlay

An article that discusses how adults can support learning and development of children through unstructured, child-led play.

The Power of Play: Learning What Comes Naturally, David Elkind

A book by a child development expert on the value of imaginative, spontaneous play.

Last Child in the Woods: Saving Our Children from Nature-Deficit Disorder, Richard Louv

An important book that has been fueling a movement by introducing studies and evidence about how direct exposure to nature is critical for children's physical and emotional development. Discover a wealth of additional research plus a growing community at Children & Nature Network.

[Playing in dirt and mud builds child's immunity](), *Child Magazine*

An article that discusses how exposure to microorganisms found outside leads to improved immune systems and how unstructured play benefits rounded-skill acquisition and development.

Why Dirt Is Good: 5 Ways to Make Germs Your Friends, Dr. Mary Ruebush

An insightful book that explores how the immune system develops in children and how you can make your immune system healthier.

Giant Mud Kitchen Photo Collection

This is the [mud kitchens Pinterest board]() I put together containing hundreds of photos of inspiring mud kitchens from around the Internet. This is a great place to get a sense of the landscape and ideas for making your own mud kitchen.

Examples and Articles of Mud Kitchens

These are links to some of the examples and articles that have inspired me along the way. Keep in mind that much of what has been published on mud kitchens represents substantially impressive designed and developed spaces, whereas my belief and experience has been that mud kitchens do not need to be elaborate or robust in order to support profound experiences for your children. I urge you to review these, but to focus on what can be accomplished within a very short span of time so you can get started immediately. You can build upon your mud kitchen, like I have over months and years.

[7 tips for mud play at preschool](), Let the Children Play

This provides helpful tips for creating larger and high-traffic play spaces.

[10 reasons why we should let children play in the mud](), Let the Children Play

Backyard Kitchen, Mama Liberated

An article that documents a quaint and perfect mud kitchen with just the basics—water, dirt, a surface, and come cookware—that kept the little one engaged for hours.

Creating a mud pie kitchen, part 1, Let The Children Play

This documents the evolution of building a mud kitchen in an unused dirt patch.

How to Set Up a Mud Pie Kitchen, TinkerLab

This is a really nice post about how to set up, test, and refine a simple mud kitchen.

Let your kids get dirty!, The Art of Simple

Five reasons dirt is healthy for kids, from boosting immune systems to building adventurous spirits.

Making a mud kitchen, Muddyfaces

This is a complete, step-by-step guide to making your own mud kitchen.

Mud, Preschool Express, by Jean Warren

This website helps you create with mud: brown as mud, mud cake, mud cake candle count, mud baths, mud bricks, "mud pudding" snacks, and more.

Mud garden—part 3, At Home with Ali

This is a thoughtful blog post documenting the design and build of a simple home mud kitchen.

Mud Pie Kitchen, Along the Way

A wonderful photo essay and tour of a romantic and iconic homemade mud pie kitchen.

<u>Mud Pie Kitchen—National Trust</u>, Adventures @ Play

This showcases a well-stocked mud pie kitchen play area at public gardens.

<u>Mud Pie Kitchen</u>, Growing a Jeweled Rose

Plan a natural, inventive, well thought out, simple mud kitchen.

<u>Mud Pie Kitchen Renovation</u>, Child Central Station

This is an awesome story that shares how the family started with a minimal mud kitchen and then, over time, slowly added furniture, fixtures, cookware, and more to make a really profoundly alluring play space.

<u>Mud Pie Kitchens Revisited</u>, Let The Children Play

Inspiring collection of mud pie kitchens, photos, and commentary.

Mud Play Ideas For Kids, Happy Hooligans

Presents a mobile mud kitchen of sorts, perfect if you don't want to make a permanent mud kitchen.

Outdoor Concoctions Kitchen, The Imagination Tree

Simple, open-ended mud kitchen and play area set up in a home garden.

Outdoor Kitchen—I have one now too!, Pre-School Play

Great example of creating a mud kitchen in an urban setting on the side of a building.

Our Mud Pie Kitchen, Teacher Tom

Innovative use of materials and space to create a multi-dimensional mud pie kitchen.

Play heats up in the outdoor kitchen, Let the Children Play

This describes cooking with wet saw dust, pebbles, twigs, leaves, seeds, and wet sand, on tires, tree slices, cupcake tins, baskets, and benches.

Shopping for Mud Pie Kitchen Accessories, TinkerLab

Shares how to find accessories for mud pie kitchens inexpensively, and their personal story of the same, including how to incorporate children into the process.

Stomping in the Mud

Natural outdoor play environment for children to play outside year-round, featuring some great snapshots of their mud kitchen.

The Mud Center: Recapturing Childhood, Community Playthings

Well-designed and developed mud center that supports a high volume of use.

We Love Mud!, Learning21

An essay about three reasons why the author loves mud and you should too.

Cheat Sheet

As much as I love books, I rarely seem to have them on me when I want to refer to them. I can't be the only person in the world who has this problem, so I made a printable 8.5"x11" cheat sheet for making your own mud kitchen. You can print it out and stick it on your fridge, in your car, or grab it when you head out of the house. To get it, email me at jason@mudkitcheninaday.com or head over to www.MudKitchenInADay.com to download (you don't have to sign up or anything—just go grab it!).

Need Help?

If you are stuck in any way, please email me at jason@mudkitcheninaday.com. So far, parents who have read this book have told me that they've been inspired to make their own outdoor play spaces and mud kitchens, which is so great. But if you're hitting a wall and need some help thinking through things, I'd love to help.

ABOUT THE AUTHOR

Jason Runkel Sperling is a husband and father to two young children. He was born and raised in Boulder, Colorado, where he currently resides, and spent his childhood exploring mountains, rivers, forests, and oceans. He is an Eagle Scout, experienced outdoorsman, has traveled in 5 continents and 45 US states, and lived in Asia and

Australia for 2 years. He has documented his outdoor adventures with his children on TheAdventureDad.com for years, founded the Running Wild Family Nature Club, and spends most of his free time trying to figure out how to increase the time his family spends outside. Professionally, Jason received his BFA from University of Colorado before completing an international MBA across three continents. He is currently the director of a software product that helps companies share their messages around the world.

If you have feedback about the book, insight as to how to make it better, or questions you wished were addressed—or just want to get in touch—you can email him at jason@mudkitcheninaday.com or visit mudkitcheninaday.com.

From the Author

Love *Mud Kitchen in a Day*? Leave a review!

I'm just getting my hands dirty (pun intended) in the world of publishing, so if you liked what you've read here, I would really appreciate you going onto Amazon to leave a review to help guide other parents. Keep in mind that the goal with this book is to move parents into action! While there is much information online about mud kitchens, I hope this book helps inspire others to get out there and start creating play spaces for their children! If you've been motivated to do so, please write a review on Amazon.com.

ALSO BY JASON RUNKEL SPERLING

UNPLUGGED

15 Steps to Disconnect from Technology and Reconnect with Nature, Yourself, Friends, and Family

Unplugged: 15 Steps to Disconnect from Technology and Reconnect with Nature, Yourself, Friends, and Family provides you with the tools that will allow you to change your parenting approach and improve your family's health, happiness, and connection.

What if a few new activities could completely transform your family? Imagine waking up in the morning feeling excited to take on the day. This book will show you how to increase your happiness, health, and connection with a few simple steps.

In his third book, Amazon bestselling author Jason Runkel Sperling covers 15 steps to improve your connection with nature, yourself, friends, and family.

Here are a few things that you will get out of Unplugged:

How to:

- Apply the Law of Attraction to help you unplug.
- Build your tribe when you're starting from zero.

- Utilize your circle of influence to inspire motivation.
- Look at your life through a victim vs. leader perspective.
- Choose to FLY when you crash.
- Employ the power of efficiency to increase your happiness.
- Disconnect from technology to focus on what really is important.
- Stay safe in a complex world.
- Conquer attachment and desire.
- Use love to build sustainable momentum.
- Emphasize small wins for big results.
- Listen to truth and generate vitality.
- Develop your audacious dreams to enrich your life.
- Discover a wise sage to guide you into nature.
- Delegate your fears and worries.

BONUS: Templates, worksheets, tips, checklists, examples, and other resources to inspire you and make taking the first step easy.

Get your copy of *Unplugged* at:

www.jasonrunkelsperling.com/unplugged.

The Backyard Play Revolution

How to Engage Kids in Simple, Inexpensive Outdoor Play and Increase Child Health and Motor/Sensory Development

In this eye-opening, easy-to-follow, action-oriented book, Jason Runkel Sperling explains how to use screen-free, unstructured outdoor play and toys to increase early-age child learning opportunities and improve happiness for the whole family.

You'll learn:

- How to encourage your child to enjoy active, outdoor, screen-free play

- How to foster unstructured, child-led playtime

- The secret to making risky play work for your child

- Practical advice on how to pick the right toys and transform your backyard

- How to set up your backyard playspace and not break the bank

- And much, much more ...

Follow one father's entertaining and informative experiments to find play and toys that inspire his children to play outside, offline, and independently—like children of past generations. Author Jason Runkel Sperling shares his six-year journey discovering the history of play, playgrounds, toys, and the role of adults in their children's experiences, culminating in a revolutionary approach to backyard play. Full of humor, parenting insight, and in-depth research, Sperling's book will change how you think about raising children, and how you organize your home.

If you're like the majority of parents today, you may have noticed the differences in modern childhood. Unlike every other generation, your children spend more time indoors, glued to screens, and are less active and free to roam than in any time in history. You likely have come across countless articles on the epidemic of child obesity and behavioral problems today, and perhaps you've heard that getting children to play outside is an easy and inexpensive remedy. You may already want to get your children to play outside, but nothing seems to motivate them. Or maybe you're frozen with fear that they might get hurt if they go out. Plus, your backyard is manicured for adult enjoyment. So instead of heading outside, your children stay indoors, damaging their health and driving you up the walls.

You may have tried lawn games, sports equipment, remote control toys, or backyard arts and crafts, but nothing seems to hold their attention. And when you do spend time in the backyard, you always have to play with them. Or, perhaps you can't stand the thought of your children not getting ahead—so the children's schedule is jam-packed with adult-led, goal-based activities outside the home. In other words, you've turned into the family chauffeur.

Whatever happened to "go outside and play?"

Raising children today is harder than ever before, but children haven't changed all that much.

The best way to get children to develop their imagination and creativity, motor and sensory skills, emotional and social intelligence, and every other physical and mental ability, is to get them to "go outside and play" with open-ended, child-led play that can be enjoyed in the backyard. There are proven, evidence-based approaches for the role parents should take in facilitating this kind of play. And you can learn them quickly and apply them tomorrow.

This doesn't mean getting rid of every after-school activity, throwing away every toy in the house, or putting the kibosh on screen time forever. But it does mean making sure that children have the active playtime necessary to prevent physical and psychological maladies. It's vital, especially with early-age children, to give them the environment and support they need to develop. You don't have to play with children every second, you just need to know the right kind of play and toys to provide, and how to gently guide them.

The Backyard Play Revolution is for parents from every background, regardless of location or income level, and is appropriate for backyards of any size.

This book isn't hundreds of pages long. You can read it quickly and take action the next day. Are you ready to profoundly impact your child's life?

Get your copy of *The Backyard Revolution* at:

www.jasonrunkelsperling.com/the-backyard-play-revolution.

Printed in Great Britain
by Amazon